T0062247

CONTENTS

Supercool Powerplant

In 2017, Amager Bakke, also known as CopenHill, opened in Copenhagen, the capital of Denmark. The building is more than an architectural wonder. It's also a power plant! Except for its 410-foot- (125-meter-) tall smoke stack, one would never even know it. The power plant burns trash from the city and turns it into low-**carbon** energy. And that's not all. CopenHill is also home to a sports center. Its 279-foot (85-m) tall slanted roof doubles as a ski slope. The slope is covered with human-made grass that is as slippery as snow. "It takes typically three runs to adjust your mind to skiing on a green dry surface," said one skier. In addition, the building has a gym and climbing wall. "We want to combine **sustainable** thinking and **innovative** architecture with recreational facilities," said Copenhagen's mayor, Frank Jensen.

CopenHill in Copenhagen, Denmark

4

CopenHill took 10 years to build from start to finish.

CopenHill cost about $600 million to construct.

CopenHill is unlike any other **industrial** building in the world. The 12-floor structure is built from glass and large metal bricks that also serve as planters. There are 7,000 bushes, 300 pine and willow trees, and various other plants covering the building. "It's so unique," said a local. "We have no mountains in Denmark. Where else can you go and have, I mean, just this view?" Two-thirds of the interior space is used for trash **incineration**. The power plant makes enough energy to heat upward of 72,000 homes per year! Bjarke Ingels is CopenHill's architect. He's passionate about sustainable and **mixed-use** architecture. "Architecture is there to give form to the future, and I'm excited that my one-year-old son will grow up in a city where it's taken for granted that you have a ski slope on top of a power plant," said Ingels.

FACT BOX

CopenHill was named World Building of the Year 2021 at the World Architecture Festival.

What Is Industrial Architecture?

What exactly is architecture? It's the art of designing buildings. And architects are the people who design buildings. When coming up with an idea for a building, architects consider shape, size, color, and materials, among other things. But this is only part of what architects do! One of their main jobs is figuring out a building's function. For example, how will a building be used? And who will use it?

Industrial architecture is a style of architecture with an important purpose. Industrial buildings are where raw materials are transformed into products. For example, industrial buildings may include power plants like CopenHill that turn waste into electricity. They may also include warehouses, **breweries**, **refineries**, and factories that make everything from cereal and clothing to cars and airplanes. The function of an industrial space is often placed above its form. However, there are many outstanding examples of industrial architecture.

FACT BOX

Architects often work with structural engineers. This type of engineer uses math and science to help design and build buildings as well as other structures like bridges.

The open floor plan of a factory that makes cars

Not all industrial buildings look the same. However, industrial architecture has some shared characteristics. For one, industrial structures tend to have open floor plans and high ceilings. This provides more space for equipment, supplies, and workers. An open floor plan and high ceiling also permit light and air to flow through a building. A bright and well-**ventilated** work environment is safer for workers.

FACT BOX

A floor plan is a diagram that shows the arrangement of rooms in a building.

Natural light is another factor that sets industrial architecture apart. Often, industrial buildings have large windows that let in a lot of light. In addition, industrial architecture is known for exposed, or visible, materials and **utilities**. For example, there may be uncovered brick walls, concrete floors, and steel beams. Ducts that carry heat and air conditioning may also be exposed, along with electrical wiring and plumbing. Finally, there is usually minimal decoration. This is called minimalism. Minimalism embraces clean lines and forms and materials that include glass, concrete, and steel.

Large windows brighten up the interior of this chemical plant. There are exposed heating and cooling ducts as well.

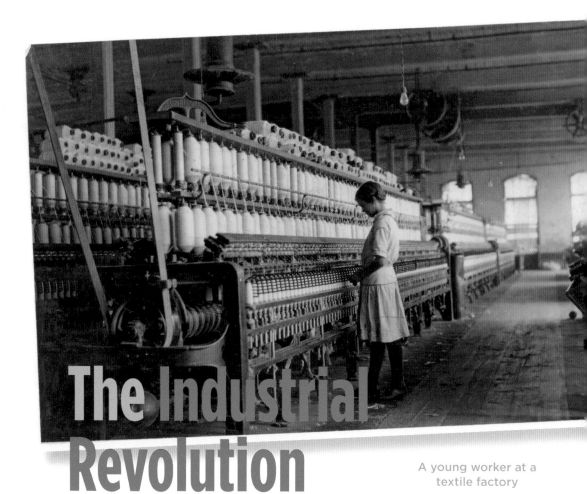

The Industrial Revolution

A young worker at a textile factory

Industrial architecture can be traced back to the 1700s in England. This was the time of the **Industrial Revolution**. Before this period, people made products by hand in small workshops. These craftspeople even made cloth by hand, which was a slow and difficult task. In 1733, an invention called the flying shuttle **revolutionized** cloth making. It made it easier and faster to weave cloth. Following the flying shuttle came the spinning jenny and **cotton gin**. Both of these inventions further sped up the cloth-making process.

Eli Whitney, the inventor of the cotton gin, also came up with the idea of machines with **interchangeable** parts. These machines could be operated by workers to produce goods. Soon, factories were built. In the late 1700s, a steam engine that could power the machines in the factories was introduced. People moved from the countryside to cities to work in factories. The factories were mostly constructed out of wood, brick, and a new building material called iron. During the 1790s, the biggest factories stood seven stories high and were often filled with thousands of busy workers.

FACT BOX

One of the earliest industrial structures is a graceful arching iron bridge in England built in 1779. It was based on a design by architect Thomas Pritchard.

The Iron Bridge is supported by five iron arches. It has some delicate decorative details.

The Industrial Revolution spread to other parts of the world. In 1825, the railroad was invented to transport new goods—and ideas. Huge structures made from iron and glass were built to house trains, markets, and various exhibitions. One of the most notable buildings of the time was the Crystal Palace, dating from 1851. **Botanist** and architect Joseph Paxton dreamed up the sprawling iron and glass structure. He used 300,000 sheets of factory-made glass and tons of iron to construct it. When it was completed, the Crystal Palace's clear glass walls and grand size amazed people. Paxton's creation was the world's first **prefabricated** building! It influenced the designs of industrial structures to come.

The Crystal Palace was originally built in Hyde Park, London, as an exhibition space. It was destroyed by a fire in 1936.

In addition to iron and glass, **reinforced** concrete and steel were introduced as building materials during this period. These extremely strong materials changed the way buildings could be built. They allowed for larger and taller

The Moulin Saulnier building is covered with a metal crisscross structure and colorful ceramic tiles.

designs. One of the first industrial buildings with external metal supports was the Moulin Saulnier building in France. It was built in 1872 as a watermill and later became a chocolate factory.

Joseph Paxton's design for the Crystal Place was inspired by the underside of a giant water lily leaf!

Factories

In the United States, the first industrial architecture was textile factories. But as new products were invented, new kinds of factories popped up. One of the most significant inventions of the late Industrial Revolution was the Model T car. Henry Ford wanted to make a car for the general public and manufacture every part of it. That way, he could produce cars efficiently and at a low price. Ford hired German-born architect Albert Kahn to design an assembly plant for his cars. In 1908, Kahn created one of the largest factories in the world in River Rouge near Detroit, Michigan.

The Model T invented by Henry Ford

This is an American factory dating from 1900. It was built by
the Solvay Process Company, a chemical producer.

The Ford River Rouge complex

For Henry Ford, it was important to build a factory where people could comfortably and safely work. So Kahn designed a building with high ceilings and towering windows that let sunlight pour into the workspaces. He also used reinforced concrete as a building material, which not only permitted larger, open work spaces but was less likely to catch fire. Kahn cared most about functionality. So, there were few decorative elements in the factory. Kahn had little time for other architects, in his words, "who attempt the **novel** just for novelty's sake."

Workers in the River Rouge Ford plant bending metal strips to form window frames for automobiles in 1941

At its peak, the Ford Rouge complex was made up of 93 buildings and nearly 16 million square feet (15 million square meters) of factory floor space. At one time, 120,000 people worked there. Kahn and his team went on to design more than 1,000 projects for Henry Ford. By 1930, it's estimated he designed 20 percent of all factory buildings in the United States!

FACT BOX

Architect Albert Kahn is known as the "father of modern factory design." He called his style the Kahn System.

Architect Albert Kahn

During the 20th century came a new modern spin on industrial architecture. German architect Peter Behrens built a factory for a **turbine** company in Berlin, Germany. Yet the building was not solely **utilitarian**. It had a bold, modern style. The concrete factory had large, stacked steel-framed windows and a curved roof that hung over the windows. Of Behrens's design, a **critic** wrote, "There is no lovelier building than that **monumental** hall of glass and reinforced concrete." More modern industrial buildings followed, including the elegant Fagus Factory, also in Germany.

Then by the middle of the 20th century, the economy changed. There was a switch from producing goods to providing services. As a result, there was less of a need for manufacturing jobs. Also, many manufacturers moved overseas to China and other countries. As a result, many U.S. industrial buildings were no longer being used. Many were abandoned. Some fell into ruin or were knocked down.

Beginning in the mid-1900s, companies began seeing industrial architecture in a different light. They no longer wanted to build lasting structures. Instead, they wanted to construct buildings cheaply and quickly.

The Fagus Factory was designed by Walter Gropius and Adolf Meyer in 1925.

Reinvented Buildings

Some industrial buildings from the 20th century avoided the wrecking ball. However, very few are still being used for industrial purposes. Incredibly, many old factories have been repurposed! They are now artist studios, offices, apartments, hotels, museums, and many other things. For example, one of Albert Kahn's old Ford factories in California is now mixed-use office space. And it's powered by the Sun's energy!

The Massachusetts Museum of Contemporary Art (MASS MoCA) is a museum in a converted factory building.

A gallery inside Dia Beacon

Dia Beacon is another example of a reinvented factory. This art museum in Beacon, New York, used to be a Nabisco box-printing factory. When the factory was open, Beacon was a thriving industrial city. Then in the 1970s, it and other factories shut down. People were left without jobs. The city fell into a slump. In 2003, the Dia Foundation turned the old box factory into one of the largest art museums in the country! Since opening, Dia Beacon has breathed new life into the city. "Dia has brought remarkable attention and **commerce** to the city of Beacon," said one of Dia's directors.

The Baltimore Design School

Similar projects are happening around the United States. An old factory in Baltimore, Maryland, was turned into a school. But not just any school. The Baltimore Design School (BDS) is a high school focusing on art, architecture, and design! The school's name is proudly displayed in large red letters across the factory's oversize windows.

FACT BOX

One challenge that architects face when repurposing old industrial architecture is transforming large, open spaces into smaller spaces that serve the needs of people today.

Before it was **renovated**, the factory building had been abandoned. It is now helping the community in multiple ways. In addition to turning an eyesore into something beautiful, it is changing lives. "My decision to go to the Baltimore Design School (BDS) has been one of the best and most influential decisions I have made thus far in my life," said a student at the school. Repurposing an old building also has less of an impact on the environment. Why? Less energy is required to adapt an old building into a new space than to build a whole new structure.

Other old industrial buildings are being used by people to create cutting-edge technology. The New Lab, in a former New York shipbuilding factory, is one such example.

In addition to repurposing old factories, architects are also designing new industrial buildings for the 21st century. One of the best examples is CopenHill. Another includes a colorful glass building in Jackson, Wyoming. Although it looks like a design center, the building is home to a **vertical** farm! Architect Nona Yehia is one of the founders of Vertical Harvest. "There's snow outside on the mountain, and we're still producing tomatoes for our community," Yehia said. The indoor farm produces 100,000 pounds (45,359 kilograms) of vegetables and other produce per year using special LED lights and trays that contain everything plants need to grow. "We're never going to replace traditional agriculture," said Yehia. But she and her company hope to bring affordable fresh produce to more Americans. Vertical Harvest has plans to build nine more green factories in cities around the country. The sky is the limit!

Design an Industrial Building

Think about what you just learned about industrial architecture in this book. Now use that information to design your own factory or other industrial building!

DESIGN CONCEPT: What is your idea for your building? What products will be made in it? Where will it be located? What materials will you use to build it? Consider your building's form *and* function.

PLAN: Think about what the exterior and interior of your building will look like. How big or small will it be? How many windows will it have?

DRAW: Grab some paper and a pencil. Sketch the floor plan of your building to show the interior space. Next, draw the exterior, noting what materials will be used.

BUILD A MODEL: Use materials around your home, such as clay, paper, cardboard, scissors, straws, popsicle sticks, and glue, to build a small model of your building.

REFINE YOUR PLAN: What works about your design? What doesn't work? Make any needed changes to improve your building.

GLOSSARY

botanist (BOT-uhn-ist) a plant expert

breweries (BROO-uh-reez) buildings that make beer or other liquors

carbon (KAR-buhn) a gas released into the atmosphere associated with climate change

commerce (KOM-ers) the activity of buying and selling on a large scale

cotton gin (KOT-uhn JIN) a machine for separating the fibers of cotton from the seeds

critic (KRIT-ik) a person who judges or criticizes something

incineration (in-SIN-uh-rey-shuhn) the process of burning something to ashes

industrial (in-DUHSS-tree-uhl) having to do with factories of businesses

Industrial Revolution (in-DUHSS-tree-uhl rev-uh-LOO-shuhn) a period in the late 1700s and early 1800s when people began to build factories and produce a large amount of goods

innovative (in-uh-VAY-tiv) having new ideas about how something can be done

interchangeable (in-ter-CHEYN-juh-buhl) two or more things that can be exchanged with each other or put in the other's place

mixed-use (MIKST-YOOS) designed for many functions

monumental (mon-yuh-MEN-tuhl) exceptionally great

novel (NOV-uhl) new or unusual in an interesting way

prefabricated (pree-FAB-rih-kety-uhd) manufactured in sections to enable assembly on site

refineries (ri-FYE-nuh-reez) factories that make oil, metals, or sugar into a usable product that can be sold to customers

reinforced (ree-in-FOHRSD) strengthened

renovated (REN-uh-veyt-uhd) restored to good condition

revolutionized (rev-uh-LOO-shuh-nahyzd) changed radically

sustainable (suh-STAYN-uh-buhl) a way of living that does not use up nonrenewable resources; living in a way that can be continued forever

turbine (TUR-bine) an engine that is powered by wind, water, or steam moving through the blades of a wheel and making it spin

utilitarian (yoo-til-ih-TAIR-ee-uhn) having usefulness over beauty

utilities (yoo-TIL-ih-teez) electricity, gas, water, and sewage

ventilated (VEN-tuh-layt-id) exposed to fresh air

vertical (VUR-tuh-kuhl) in an up-and-down direction

READ MORE

Allen, Peter. *Atlas of Amazing Architecture*. London: Cicada Books, 2021.

Armstrong, Simon. *Cool Architecture*. London: Pavilion, 2015.

Dillon, Patrick. *The Story of Buildings*. Somerville, MA: Candlewick Press, 2014.

Glancey, Jonathan. *Architecture: A Visual History*. London: DK, 2021.

Moreno, Mark. *Architecture for Kids*. Emeryville, VA: Rockridge Press, 2021.

LEARN MORE ONLINE

Architecture for Children
https://archforkids.com

Britannica Kids: Architecture
https://kids.britannica.com/students/article/architecture/272939

Center for Architecture: Architecture at Home Resources
https://www.centerforarchitecture.org/k-12/resources/

Lego Design Challenge
https://www.architects.org/uploads/BSA_LWW_LEGO_Challenge.pdf

STEAM Exercises: Kid Architecture
http://www.vancebm.com/kidArchitect/pages/steamExercises.html

INDEX

ABOUT THE AUTHOR

Joyce Markovics has written hundreds of books for young readers. She lives in a nearly 200-year-old carpenter Gothic style house along the Hudson River. Joyce would like to thank architect, designer, and city planner Jeff Shumaker for his insight and help creating this series.

BUILDING BIG INDUSTRIAL
ARCHITECTURE

People have been designing different types of buildings for thousands of years! Each structure was built using architecture—an amazing combination of science and art. This series explores different styles of architecture and takes an up-close look at some remarkable buildings and the architects who designed and built them.

....

Read all these Building Big titles:

Ancient Architecture

Classical Architecture

Green Architecture

Industrial Architecture

Modern Architecture

Smart Architecture

GR: V

ISBN-13: 978-1668920862

9 781668 920862

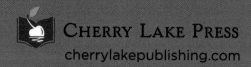

CHERRY LAKE PRESS

cherrylakepublishing.com